Prayers
for
College
Students

To chuck
With our prayers
& love
mom & DJ

Christmas '83

PRAYERS

FOR COLLEGE STUDENTS

JAMES T. CUMMING
HANS MOLL

CONCORDIA

Publishing House
St. Louis

*We dedicate this book to the glory of God,
with special thanks to our loving wives*

Margaret Ann Cumming
and
Marcia Lucille Moll

Biblical references are from the Revised Standard Version of the Bible, copyrighted 1946, 1952, © 1971, 1973. Used by permission.

Manufactured in the United States of America

Library of Congress Cataloging in Publication Data

Cumming, James T., 1938-
 Prayers for college students.

 1. College students—Prayer-books and devotions—English. I. Moll,
Hans, 1938-   . II. Title. BV4850.C85 1982   242'.634   82-8283
ISBN 0-570-03869-3

1 2 3 4 5 6 7 8 9 10   CB   91 90 89 88 87 86 85 84 83 82

Contents

CONTENTS 7

Dear Reader,

For you who use this book of prayers we offer: "Grace to you and peace from God our Father and the Lord Jesus Christ" (Philippians 1:2).

In this book you will find prayers dealing with many special concerns and problems of college age students. The prayer topics are based on questions raised by young people in the books *Hey, God, What About...?* (Concordia, 1977) and *And, God, What About...?* (Concordia, 1980), by the authors, and the ideas and suggested prayers of the college students listed on the "Acknowledgments" pages.

Some of the prayers employ the A. C. T. S. (Adoration, Confession, Thanks, and Supplication) format described in Section I. Other prayers use only one, two, or three facets of that scheme. We suggest that you use the prayers offered as they are, that you adopt the A.C.T.S. format, and that you use the prayer topics to compose your own prayers.

We thank Linda Smith for the excellent typing of the manuscript. Special gratitude and love is expressed to our wives, Marcia and Margaret, and our children, Amy, Carol, Christine, David, Debra, Emily, and Heidi, for their help, constructive criticism, support, and understanding during the months of preparation of this work. We, of course, also thank our Father in heaven for what He has taught us about prayer during our study and work together, and do so in Jesus' wonderful name. Amen.

James T. Cumming
Hans Moll

Acknowledgments

We sincerely thank the following individuals for the time, the ideas, and the suggested prayers they contributed. We pray that their efforts will be a blessing to students who follow them.

Concordia College, River Forest, Ill.:
Brenda Barry
Lori Barsema
Dorcas Ernst
Karon Hammond
Monte Haun
Donna Kirst
Lori Sauder
Southern Illinois University, Carbondale, Ill.:
Margaret Cumming
University of Illinois, Urbana, Ill.:
Brice Rosendale
University of Wisconsin, La Crosse, Wis.:
Dawn Bennett
Gary Franke
Christine Halvorson
Valparaiso University, Valparaiso, Ind.:
Allison Eckhardt
Jody Geerdes
Kirsten Johnson
Tim Meinzen
Heidi Moll
Marcia Moll

Sherry O'Connor
John Rudy
Kimberly Spees
Waubonsee Community College, Sugar Grove, Ill.:
Lois Draves
Western Illinois University, Macomb, Ill.:
Arlene Ahrens
Julie Brown
Michael Burdick
Janice Fata
Karen Koppen
Marty Mainzer
Vivian Nelson
Lori Proudfoot
George Remus
Lisa Ruff
Dale Wohlers
Margie Zeedyk

Western Wisconsin Technical Institute, La Crosse, Wis.
Albert Hogen

Introduction
to
Prayers

O come, let us sing to the Lord;
    let us make a joyful noise to the rock of our
       salvation!
Let us come into His presence with thanksgiving;
    let us make a joyful noise to Him with songs
       of praise! . . .
O come, let us worship and bow down,
    let us kneel before the Lord, our Maker!

Psalm 95:1-2, 6

"Hear My Prayer, O God"

God, our Father, listens to the prayers His children address to Him. He hears what we say to Him in Jesus' name. The God of the Bible hears our words as well as our thoughts and inner desires. Prayer is the means by which we submit ourselves and our requests to our loving Father. Jesus has invited us to speak to our heavenly Father in prayer. Therefore we can be confident God does hear us and will do what is best for us.

When Jesus' first disciples asked Him to teach them how to pray, He taught them the model prayer we now call the Lord's Prayer. In this prayer Jesus gives us a beautiful and concise example to follow. By His life Jesus also showed us how to lead a life of prayer. As you read the Gospels, note how often and in what situations Jesus talked to His (and our) Father in prayer.

There are a variety of literary forms used in prayers. There are many ways to express ourselves in prayer. There are many and varied subjects about which to pray. Many of the forms of prayer, the ways of expressing prayer, and the subjects of prayer are used by Christians in their church services. When we worship together it is customary for us to begin and conclude our services with silent prayer. Then in prayers using the forms of hymns, chants, and unison readings we invoke God's presence, we ask for His forgiveness, we praise His name, and we ask for His blessings. When the pastor leads us in prayer we express our concurrence by singing or speaking an "Amen."

God through the apostle Paul urges us to "pray constantly" (1 Thessalonians 5:17). Does this mean we should always have our heads bowed and our hands folded in prayer? Does this mean we should never have any thoughts but prayer? That hardly seems possible. The apostle reminds us we can speak to God anywhere and at any time. He would have us realize prayers can be both brief and unspoken. He would have us adopt an *attitude* of prayer. Our prayers to God need not be long or formal. They need not be original or *ex corde*. They should be spoken or thought with the confidence that our Father in heaven will hear and answer our prayers.

The Christian uses a variety of prayer forms in a variety of ways. The content of our prayers includes words of adoration, words of confession of sin, words of thanks, and words of supplication. The acronym A.C.T.S. helps us remember these four important aspects of prayer. The Christian regularly uses these aspects of prayer in his or her personal devotional life.

Adoration of God is a good way to begin a prayer. We praise and glorify Him for what He is and what He has done. "Hallelujah," which means "Praise Jehovah," is a one-word prayer of adoration. When we adore God, we make it known that He is worthy to be held in honor. He who is eternal, unchangeable, omnipotent, omniscient, omnipresent, holy, just, and yet all-merciful surely is the One we want to adore.

When we approach God in prayer, we do not do so on the basis of any righteousness in us. We know we cannot stand before Him on what we have been and/or what we have done. This is why another important aspect of prayer is the *confession* of sin. The tax collector in the temple simply prayed, "God be merciful to me a sinner" (Luke 18:13b). Confession is good for the soul. It is good for us to get the sins that are bothering us off our chests. In a prayer of confession we humble ourselves before God. When we do, we need to remember there is forgiveness with the Lord for all our sins. He will raise up those who are bowed down; He will not break the bruised reed (Isaiah 42:1-4).

After we lay our sins on Jesus, the precious Lamb of God, we can thank God for the blessings He gives. *Thanksgiving* is the joy-filled heart of a prayer. God lavishes His blessings on us; in prayer we respond by thanking Him for blessings, both great and small. As a parent is pleased when we say, "thank you," how much more will our heavenly Father be pleased when we thank Him.

In our *supplications* to God, we include requests for ourselves and for others. Our God and Father wants us to call on Him in every trouble. None of our needs is too insignificant for Him to consider. None of our petitions is too difficult for Him to grant. We pray with confidence that He will give us those things He has promised us in the Bible. However, when we ask Him about matters He has not revealed to us in His holy Word, we submit ourselves and our will to Him with the phrase, "If it is Your will." We do not issue demands to God. We do not tell Him how and when He should answer our prayers. In our supplications we have the opportunity to do something positive about our concerns for others. We can intercede for both our friends and our enemies. We can, also, be certain the Holy Spirit helps us in our weaknesses, even when we do not know what to say.

Our prayer for this book and for you is:
Our all-knowing Father and God,
accept us, our words, and our sincere desires for this book.
Please send Your Spirit to the users of this book so they
    may draw closer to You.
We pray in Jesus' wonderful name. Amen.

Prayers
for the
Week

Make a joyful noise to the Lord, all the lands!
Serve the Lord with gladness!
   Come into His presence with singing! ...
Enter His gates with thanksgiving,
   and His courts with praise!
   Give thanks to Him, bless His name!

Psalm 100:1-2, 4

Beginning of the Day

Lord, thank You for guarding me through the night,
And keep me always within Your sight.
And now in this day I'm about to begin,
Guard me from evil and temptation to sin.
Amen, Jesus, hear me.

End of the Day

Lord, thank You for guiding me through this day,
    And please forgive me the sins I have committed along
        the way.
Help me, by Your Spirit, to stay close by Your side,
    And as I travel the road of life, my God, be my Guide.
Amen, Jesus, hear me.

Lord's Day Morning

I begin this first day of a new week in the same way my
spiritual life began, in the name of the Father, and of the
Son, and of the Holy Spirit.

This is the day, O Lord, which You have made and given to me. I dedicate it and myself to You and Your praise. Hallelujah!

As I begin this first day of the week, I am reminded that I have not kept the First Table of Your Law. I have not loved You with all my heart, soul, and mind. I am convicted of my sins against Your commandment not to put other gods before You. Forgive me, Father. Forgive me also for taking and/or condoning the taking of Your holy name in vain. I am sorry I have not kept Your commandment against this. I am also ashamed to admit some of my worship during the past week has been vain repetition. I have not always worshiped You in spirit and in truth. Forgive me for breaking Your commandment which demands sincere worship. I confess my sins and I ask You to wash me and cleanse me from within.

Thank You, Father, for giving me this Lord's Day so I might have a fresh opportunity to praise You in Your home among Your people. During this very hour bless all of those who are preparing to lead me in worship and teach me Your Word. Equip them all with Your Spirit of truth, power, and love. Then when we praise You together, accept the sacrifices of thanksgiving we offer You in our Lord Jesus' name. Amen.

Lord's Day Evening

My Lord, this has been a wonderful day. I really enjoyed it. Accept my heartfelt thanks for giving it to me.

Thanks also for leading me to worship and study among people who really love You and are sincerely concerned about me and other college students. I was moved by the contributions made by our organist and choir members. I sincerely appreciate the warmth the leaders and the people of _______________________________ _______ Church show to me and my fellow students.

Thanks for the words of truth, love, and encouragement You provided through Pastor _____________________ . He is a man after Your own heart. Continue to bless his ministry among us. Support him and keep him steadfast in Your Word.

Hear my special intercession for the members of my family back home. I pray they may have put themselves into Your praise so that their worship may have been as exciting as mine was today. Protect and prosper them in their endeavors during this new week.

I have seen a few of my friends who have just returned from spending the weekend at home. Thanks, Father, for granting them Your protection in both directions on their trip. Now bless us all with a good night's sleep so we will all rise to be faithful stewards of the time You give us in class and at study.

Good night, Father. I commit my soul to Your safe-keeping in Jesus' name. Amen.

Weekday Morning I

Good morning, holy Father, holy Son, and Holy Spirit: Thank You for the gift of a good night's sleep. Accept my "Hallelujah!"

Forgive my unclean thoughts since we last communicated.

O Lord, I have a busy week ahead of me. Please help me. I ask You to:

protect me from physical harm;
help me with the term paper which is due soon;
help me keep my mind on my studies as I prepare for the
    exam scheduled for the end of the week;
assist me to understand the lectures of the professor who
    always confuses me;
show me how to make new friends with those in class;
keep me from fighting with my roommate; and
help me always to remember why I am here at school.

These matters, as well as other needs I have, please grant to me in Your own way and in Your own time. I submit myself and my will to Your will because I trust in Jesus. Hear me for His holy name's sake. Amen.

Weekday Morning II

"Praise God, from whom all blessings flow;
Praise Him, all creatures here below;
Praise Him above, ye heavenly hosts;
Praise Father, Son, and Holy Ghost. Amen."

The older I get, dear Father, the more I am impressed with the depth of meaning the hymnist offers in the common doxology. The more I learn of Your vast and impressive creation, the more I can praise You. Please continue to give me more knowledge as well as true wisdom as I mature in Your service.

Dear Creator and Dispenser of time, it is already the middle of the week. Forgive me for killing or wasting the precious time You have given me. Make me a careful steward of the hours of this day, and the hours of the rest of the week.

Father, send me the Spirit of Your Son, so that I may be

an effective witness to Your mercy during this day. Guide me to build up my brothers and sisters in Christ. Enable me by my conduct to prepare the way for those who do not know the love of Jesus. Help me live up to my high calling as Your child, so that I will not give offense to any lost person or weak Christian. Then give me or someone else the opportunity to share the Good News of Jesus with those who are still enslaved in sin. Bless all Biblical evangelism endeavors in accordance with Your desire that all human beings may be saved and come to the knowledge of the truth in Jesus.

According to Your good pleasure, help me enjoy periods of relaxation during this day, and help me efficiently use my periods of study.

I pray in Jesus' name because I believe and confess that He lives and rules with the Father and the Spirit as one God forever. Amen.

Weekday Evening I

Ever-present Help in every trouble, hear these few words at the end of another day. I praise You as my almighty, omniscient, eternal, and all-gracious Father. Accept me and accept my expressions of gratitude for being my Refuge and my Strength.

I am ashamed, for I led one of my brothers/sisters in Jesus astray today. I stole the time he/she should have spent studying. Your commandment against stealing convicts me as a thief. I plead for forgiveness for the sake of Jesus, the Savior of all sinners.

Permit this forgiven sinner to thank You, Father, for

the way You have been helping my roommate and me get along. Things are improving between us.

Infinite God, please also accept the praise I offer to You for the little bit of knowledge You have given me. There is so much to learn; please help me assimilate as much as I can during these days at college.

Thanks also for the eager mind You have given me. You are so good, and Your majesty and mercy endure forever. That is why I address You in Jesus' saving name. Amen.

Weekday Evening II

My Father, Refuge of the weary, I am tired.
My Jesus, I accept Your invitation to come to You for rest.
My Comforter, revive my spirit.

Dear God, it has been a long, hard week, and I am bushed as I lie down tonight.

But before I fall asleep, I wish to thank You for a wonderful day. I think I did well on that big test. ________________________ is a great person. We had a good time tonight with our friends. I thank You, God, for all my friends.

According to Your promise, give me, Your beloved, restful sleep. I submit myself to You in the name of Jesus, Your beloved and mine. Amen.

Saturday Morning

O Creator of all that is good, I worship You with all honor and trust in Your Son. I am pleased to know that You have been my fathers' God and that You will be my children's God. I acknowledge that You are holy, eternal, unchangeable, omnipotent, omnipresent, and omniscient as well as all-merciful.

Again You have fulfilled Your promise to bless me with rejuvenating sleep. You have fearfully and wonderfully made me. Forgive me for overdoing it and for abusing my body with insufficient sleep. Bless me as this day I rest as You did on the last day of the creation week (Genesis 2:1-3).

Although I have been looking forward to this weekend in order that I may take it easy, don't let me be lazy. Do not permit me to just "kill time." Make me a faithful steward of Your precious gift of time.

Eternal Father, I speak to You in the name of Jesus, Your eternal Son. Amen.

Saturday Evening

Holy God, You have heard all my vows of faithfulness, You have listened to all my prayers, and You have seen how I have fallen short of both Your expectations for me and my expectations for myself.

During this week, I know, I have not measured up to the standard of Your perfect Law. Tonight I am thinking about the commandments at the end of the Decalog.

Have I spoken or listened to false witnesses against my neighbor? Have I enjoyed the gossip I heard about _________________ ? I am sorry to admit I have. Forgive me, merciful Father.

Have I coveted or wished to have what rightfully belongs to my neighbor? Have I been greedy? I have. Cleanse me thoroughly, Jesus, Savior, and make me clean within. Then send me Your strong Spirit so I will be able to amend my sinful life and serve You with holy works.

At the end of this day and this week, I am looking forward to the excitement of praising You with Your saints at ____ Church. Now I close this week in the same way as I began it, in the name of God the Father, the Son, and the Holy Spirit. Amen.

Prayers
for the
Church Year

Bless the Lord, O my soul;
    and all that is within me,
    bless His holy name!
Bless the Lord, O my soul,
    and forget not all His benefits,
who forgives all your iniquity,
    who heals all your diseases,
who redeems your life from the Pit . . .
(Psalm 103:1-4a)

Advent

Lord Jesus Christ, I praise You for coming into time for me and my salvation. I thank You for making known to me in my time Your full and free forgiveness. I am grateful to You for the revelation of Your grace by Your Spirit in Your Word. O divine Savior, guide me to use this Advent season to prepare myself and others for Your glorious advent at the end of time.

My dear Father, even though You have not seen fit to reveal to Your people when Your Son will come again in glory, renew in me the confidence in Your promise that He will come again. By Your abiding Word, make me ever ready and set to go when He comes again to be the judge of the living and the dead. Fill me with Your Spirit, O God, so I might live in repentance and walk by faith all the days You give me. My Father, I pray with all that is within me, that Your kingdom of grace will come to many of my contemporaries so they will not be swept away as so many people were in the days of Noah. May Your kingdom of glory come soon.

Come, Lord Jesus. Come quickly. Amen.

Christmas

Happy birthday, Jesus my Brother, happy birthday to You!

Dear Jesus, always impress on me that You loved me enough to willingly become like me in every way, except that You were neither sinful nor a sinner. I praise You for giving Yourself to buy my freedom from the slavery of sin. You became and are my relative who redeemed me. Your love for me is far beyond my ability to comprehend fully. I realize I cannot understand how You could become the Babe of Bethlehem and still be God of God and Light of Light. Help me, Lord, to realize that Your eternal love is so great it transcends all my disappointments, all my shortcomings, all my sorrows, and all my fears for the future.

Remind me, our Father and Jesus' Father, that absolutely nothing will ever be able to separate me from Your love in Jesus. You have told me that in Your holy Word. Bless me, so I will always trust in Your Word.

In Christ, the Savior, I pray. Amen.

New Year

My Father, the Creator of time, I thank You for the many days, months, and years You have given me. This is one of Your very valuable gifts.

I beg Your forgiveness for the time I have wasted during the past year. I know I can never recover the time that has been lost. I am really sorry for what I have done, especially when I "killed time." I ask You, my Father, to make me wiser than I have been. Make me a better steward of the time You entrust to me in the coming year.

At the beginning of this new year I give myself to You, O Lord, in Jesus' name. I ask that You will always guide me with Your eye, and that Your ears will always be open to my prayers.

For me to live is Christ, and this is why I speak to You in His saving name. Amen.

Epiphany

O Jesus, Sun of Righteousness, I thank You for shining on me with Your light and warmth. You have dispelled the darkness and dire consequences of my sins.

Light of my life, grant that I will be an efficient reflector of You and Your love in this dark world. I am aware that many people are still living in the darkness of sin and in the shadow of death. They do not know that You, the Light, have come. Make me a light to them so that they will be attracted to Your salvation. For those who still live out in the cold, send me, send someone, to warm them with Your love, my beautiful Savior.

Dear Jesus, hear me. Amen.

Lent

During this Lenten season, O Lord, grant that my spirit may mature more than my body. Let me appreciate as I never have before the great eternal love Jesus demonstrated on the way to the cross. Do not let me forget that Jesus loved me so much that He fulfilled the Law and suffered for me.

Jesus, I am a sinner. I thank You for taking my place under the Law, as well as for taking my place on the cross. I have benefited from both Your active obedience and Your passive obedience. You have set me free from the consequences of my sin. You are a wonderful Redeemer.

Enable me to take my stand on Jesus, the solid rock, in the realization that *all* other ground is sinking sand. Jesus, Your blood and righteousness plead for me. Amen.

Maundy Thursday

Lord Jesus Christ, my only Savior, I give thanks to You that on this night You first prepared for me the wonderful means of grace which is Holy Communion. Bless me as I prepare to dine with You tonight. You are a very gracious Host. You have set a festive board for me.

Grant that as I examine myself before eating and drinking at Your table I will see that in and of myself I am not worthy to be Your guest. Yet, make me realize anew how You have invited me by Your boundless grace. Assure me again that I can come to this holy meal in a worthy manner when I trust in You and Your Word. I do believe Your Word, Jesus. When I eat *this* bread and drink from *this* cup, I do receive Your very body and blood. I believe I receive the same for the forgiveness of all my sins.

With this real blessing I am convinced my trust in You will be strengthened and my commitment to You will be deepened.

With my fellow believers I recall how You sacrificed Yourself as our Passover Lamb. Fill me with Your Spirit so I will demonstrate my love for You by loving others the way You have loved me. Give us more of Your Spirit, dear Jesus, so we will act upon the mandate to love one another as You loved us. Counsel us with the Spirit of truth, so we might find newer and better ways to serve each other.

In Your saving name, Lord Jesus, I pray. Amen.

Good Friday

Jesus the Christ, grant that on this Good Friday I see again how terrible sin really is. I recognize that my sins caused You to be nailed to the tree of the cross. I am truly sorry. Forgive me.

Also grant this day that I may gain a new sense of the greatness of Your forgiveness. Fill me with Your grace, Your Spirit, and Your mind so that I may have and enjoy the peace that surpasses all my understanding in You.

My dear Redeemer, thank You for making this "good for me" Friday. Amen.

Resurrection Sunday

My risen and reigning Lord and Savior, I am very grateful to You for willingly laying down Your life as a ransom for me. I know on this resurrection day that You possess the power both to lay down Your life and the power to take it up again.

You, my Redeemer, have demonstrated that You met our archenemy and have conquered him. You have won the victory over sin, sorrow, death, and the devil, *and* You have given that victory to me and all believers.

I give You most hearty thanks for turning our sorrow over sin into the joy and peace of forgiveness. Lord Jesus, You are my joy and my salvation. I now have life in the Father, and communion with Your Spirit. Keep me in Your care and in Your Word so that I will always walk by faith.

On this day of resurrection I thank You for the lives, the witness, and the fruits of faith which You have given me through beloved friends and relatives who are now asleep in Your arms. Give me the same blessed death You gave them, and ever remind me that You will bring all of us with You when You come again in glory.

You, Jesus, are my resurrection and my life. Yes, Lord, I believe in You. Amen.

Pentecost

On this anniversary of the day of Pentecost I praise You, my Father in heaven, for pouring out Your Spirit on me and all my brothers and sisters who call Jesus Savior and Lord. I am pleased You have shown me, through both the prophets of the Old Testament and the apostles of the New Testament, that Jesus ushered in the last days.

In these last days give me and all my brothers and sisters the confidence to look forward now to Jesus' return in glory. Do not let my heart be filled with fear when I see the signs and wonders You are showing in the heavens and on earth. Rather, fill me with the assurance that *nothing* can separate me from Your love for me in Jesus.

O Spirit of the Father and of the Son, so fill me with Yourself that I will share the love of Jesus with all. O Lord, help me to help others so they too will call on Your name and be saved forevermore.

It is in the saving name of Jesus that I pray. Amen.

Trinity

Blessed Holy Trinity, since the beginning of the Advent season the liturgical forms used in corporate worship have made me aware of the great things You have done for me. I know You have done them for me not because I am good but because You are good. During the festival half of the church year I have benefited from these reminders of how merciful You are.

Now that the paraments in the chancel have all been changed to green, I am reminded that You want me to be a productive branch on Jesus, the true vine. Therefore renew my spirit so I might bear much good fruit. Let others see my good works and give glory to You for whom I live. Use everything I do and say to demonstrate that You are a wonderful Lord. Let the love of Christ so control me that others will come to the realization of You as a wonderful God and so meet You in the person of Jesus.

In His grace-filled name I pray. Amen.

Reformation

God the Father, I glorify You as the source of all truth.

God the Son, I thank You for being the One who has revealed in Your person and in Your work the Father's truth.

God the Holy Spirit, I praise You as the Spirit of truth who leads us into all truth.

Blessed Holy Trinity, please hear me as I call to You on this Reformation day. I call to You from "the depths," as this is a time of doctrinal indifference. Never let me succumb to the temptation to teach anything less than *Your* holy and power-filled Word. Always move me to strap on the sword of the Spirit, the Word of God. Teach me to use it in such a way that I, and others around me, will be convicted of our sins and comforted by Your Good News. Grant that as I speak Your Word of truth I will do so with great patience and with careful instruction.

Sustain me, Lord Jesus, that I might be as consistent and persistent in my witness to You as Martin Luther and other Reformation leaders were. Support me when You ask me to suffer for righteousness' sake. Bless me so I might be a blessing to others.

Ever reform your church, dear Redeemer, and begin with me. Amen.

When You
Pray
Alone

I cry with my voice to the Lord,
    with my voice I make supplication to the Lord,
I pour out my complaint before Him,
    I tell my trouble before Him.
(Psalm 142:1-2)

First Day on Campus

My God, Father, Son, and Holy Spirit, I thank and praise You for allowing me to pass this significant milestone in my life, this first day on the campus of _______________________________ (name of college). You are indeed the Lord of my life.

I thank You:

for the opportunities I will have to learn about Your
    marvelous creation while I am enrolled here;

for the many and varied occasions I will have to serve You;

for the teachers and staff who will provide the human side
    of my education;

for the friendships I will make during the years ahead; and

for the opportunities I will have to develop the talents with
    which You have endowed me.

My Lord, I must admit I was afraid to leave home. I am afraid of the unknown. I pray, be with me so I will learn to feel as secure here and wherever You would lead me as I do at home. Give me Your love, Your guidance, and Your protection in the years ahead.

I pray in Jesus' name and ask You to hear me for His sake. Amen.

Last Day on Campus

Holy Father, Holy Son, Holy Spirit, we have made it. Today I am graduating. I thank and praise You for allowing me to pass this significant milestone in my life, this last day on the campus of _________________________ (name of college). Your love, Your guidance, and Your protection have enabled me to succeed. You are indeed the Lord of my life.

I thank You:

for the opportunities I have had to learn so much about Your vast universe since I have been a student here;

for the ways You have permitted me to serve You and those You love;

for the teachers and staff who have taught and counseled me;

for the wonderful friendships I have formed;

for the opportunities I have had to develop the talents with which You have endowed me; and for the job I will begin in the near future.

My Lord, You remember how afraid I was to leave home. Well, now I am a bit afraid to leave this place. I feel secure here. Yet I am confident that You, to whom the future belongs, will be with me in the years ahead. Continue, as You have in the past, to give me Your love, Your guidance, and Your protection as long as I live.

I pray in Jesus' name and ask You to hear me for His sake. Amen.

Freshman's Prayer

In the name of the Father, and of the Son, and of the Holy Spirit. Amen.

Be with me, Father, and hold me tight. Support me, the way You support all things, with Your Word of power. I feel so alone in this strange place. I feel so out-of-place. I have been here a while and yet I am still, at times, uncomfortable. When I have been home for a weekend I feel strange also.

My parents seem different somehow. Neither they nor my friends back home seem to understand me any longer. I look forward to going home, but when I am there I look forward to returning to campus. Then when I get back, I find some people here are distant and uncaring. I have mixed feelings about this place and about myself. My Father, do not forsake me.

My Jesus, thank You for sticking closer to me than a brother. I thank You for the bond of Christian love that has drawn me close to _________________________ (name of person) and to other new friends I have met since coming here. I must admit I am enjoying the challenge of those interesting classes. I am also enjoying my new freedom. As I try new and exciting things, protect me; give me the protection of Your ministering spirits, the angels.

My Counselor sent by the Father and the Son, pick me up when I am down and guide me when I am perplexed. Show me the way to go when I am not sure what I should do. Guide me that I may use the freedom I enjoy in Jesus, not to do evil but to do good. Assist me in prayer, particularly when I do not know for what I should pray. Help me, Holy Spirit, as I pray in Jesus' wonderful name. Amen.

Sophomore's Prayer

Omniscient God and Father, teach me Your ways and show me Your truth.

Merciful Lord, forgive me for straying from the way of peace. Forgive me for offending You in many and varied ways during my first year away from home. Grant that I may have learned from the mistakes I have made, and help me to avoid places and situations in which it will be so easy to sin.

Blessed Savior, I thank You for changing what was once such a strange and uncomfortable place into my new "home." I now feel I belong here. Thanks for the caring friends You have sent into my life. Thanks for helping me in my academic work. Enable me to look realistically at my talents and interests so I will choose a major that will suit me well. I want to use all the talents and interests You have given me to Your glory.

Holy Spirit, my Counselor, even though I am now a sophomore, do not permit me to be sophomoric. I have learned a few things, but I ask You to help me realize how much more there is to learn. Keep me humble and lead me to study and to serve Jesus in all I do.

In His grace-filled name I pray. Amen.

Junior's Prayer

Lord God of hosts, the architect of the universe and the admiral of the Christian fleet, I praise You for caring so much for me. What am I among all You have made? I know You care for me. You sent Your Son to live and die for me. I know You will guide me; You have given me Your Spirit in the Word.

My God, I am grateful to You for helping me navigate through the wide-open and rough seas of my first two years of school. I recognize my chart and compass come from You. You have made it possible for me to set my course with a major and minors. Help me stick to this course. Be with me so I will be able to fulfill all the requirements for graduation on time.

My Lord, You know I have been looking for a "first mate" to sail with me. I have not found him/her yet. I ask

You to guide me to the one You have in mind for me. Make this person someone after Your own heart.

Jesus, captain of my soul and Lord of my life, sail with me so that I will reach the safe harbor of heaven. Lord Jesus, hear my prayer. Amen.

Senior's Prayer

O eternal God, I have learned from Your holy Word that You know the future better than I know either the present or the past. Therefore, although I am unable to see very far down the road of my life, I am willing to put my hand in Your hand and let You lead me.

My Lord, while my last year at college is fruitful and exciting, I must admit that since I do not yet have a job I am worried. As I fill out job applications, lead me to throw all my anxieties on You. Do not let me be disappointed when I do not "hear," as soon as I would like, about a job I think I should get. While it seems to me that my future is uncertain, do not let me become depressed.

Support me with Your loving kindness, dear Father.

Counsel me with Your Word, Holy Spirit.

Make me free indeed, Jesus, my Brother. Amen.

Confession

O God, be merciful to me.

I am a sinner.

I am not proud of myself, and

I humble myself under Your mighty and righteous hand.

My sins and my guilt get me down.

Therefore I plead for Your forgiveness.
    Wash me thoroughly.
    Cleanse me of all my sins, and
    Blot out all my transgressions.
    Make me clean on the inside as well as the outside.
    Raise me up.
Please do so for Jesus' sake, the Righteous One.
    He gave His life for me,
    He took my sins to the cross with Him,
    He loves me, and
    He bids me pray for forgiveness in His name.
That's what I am doing right now.
Father, forgive me for Jesus' sake. Amen.

Before Holy Communion

Jesus, my gracious Host, I thank You very much for the invitation You have extended to me to dine with You at Your holy table. I know You want me to come not because I am so good but because You are so good. Give me a full measure of Your Spirit so that I will carefully examine myself as I prepare to commune with You.

Let me see again the rottenness of my sins. Don't just let me lament them, but help me change my mind about my less-than-perfect thoughts, words, and deeds. Enable me to be truly repentant for every sin. Then, dear Savior, deepen my trust in You.

As I look forward to partaking again of Holy Communion, I ask You to renew in me the confidence that in this Holy Supper You will give me some things I cannot see. You have said that You give me Your body and blood as well as the forgiveness of all my sins. Lord, I believe. Help me overcome my unbelief. Grant that, with sincere trust in You and Your Word, I may eat of Your bread and drink of Your cup in a worthy manner. Strengthen my faith in You so that I may serve You and all You love with gladness all the days of my life. For me to live is Christ, and this is why I beg You to hear my fervent prayer. Amen.

After Holy Communion

Lord Jesus, I have again tasted Your mercy, and I know that You are good. Your mercy does endure forever.

As I leave Your table I am pleased to know I have again proclaimed Your redeeming death. Grant that I will have the privilege of doing so again many times before You come again in glory. Permit me to witness in other ways to what a wonderful Savior You are. May this food for my soul equip me to live by faith in You, to amend my sinful life, and to produce fruits of faith which will endure forever. Grant that all I do on campus will be to our Father's glory.

Let me depart from Your table in peace and joy. Let me love life and see good days. I have great expectations of You, Jesus, as I live and pray in Your saving name. Amen.

Homesickness

O God, I am homesick.
    I feel so alone.
    I am frightened, and I feel so unsure about myself.
    I am afraid of many things in this new place.
O my Father, I wish I were back home.
    I would like to take off and run home.
    I miss the warmth and the security of my home.

I miss my mom and dad, and even my brothers and sisters.
I would like to pet my cat and talk to my dog.
Oh, how I wish I could be with my old friends again.
It would be so great just to sit around and talk with them
about the good times we had together.
Where are all these people now?
What are they doing?
Are they thinking about me?
Oh, how I wish I were back home again!
O my Lord, I'd go home this weekend if it weren't for those
exams I have first thing Monday morning. I know I
must stay here this weekend.
O Creator and Giver of time, guide me so I will use the hours
of this weekend carefully. When I am studying, help me
to concentrate on what I am doing. Do not let my mind
wander. Help me to get so involved in important
matters that I will not have time to feel sorry for myself.
When Your day, the Lord's day, comes, draw me by Your
Spirit to join Your people in worship. Grant that I may
do my part to build up my brothers and sisters in Jesus.
By Your holy Word and at Your holy table remind me
that I am not alone.
O Jesus, assure me (and do it over and over again) that You
will never leave me nor forsake me. Remind me of Your
promise to be with me always. Give me the peace that
surpasses all understanding. Let Your angels stand
sentry duty over me, My Lord and my Savior. Amen.

Loneliness

Great God, I feel so alone.
The people around me seem so distant.
The days seem so long, and the nights even longer.
Even You seem far away.

Gracious Savior, I am feeling sorry for myself again.
   Please forgive me for being so self-centered.
   Reassure me of Your presence and of Your love.
   Remind me again of Your promise to be with me
      always.
   Revive my faith, my love, and my joy.
Comforting and powerful Spirit, build me up in Your grace.
   Equip me with Your might.
   Give me the endurance I need to bear up under
      loneliness.
   Give me Your peace.
   Lift me up in Jesus' name, and for Jesus' sake.
   Amen.

Help Me Make New Friends

Since You, Lord my Shepherd, have led me to this new school, I ask You to help me make new friends. You have promised to be my ever-present help in every trouble and every need. In Jesus, You have promised to hear me when I call to You.

Even though I know You will never leave me nor forsake me, I must admit that since I have been here I have been lonely. I miss my friends at home. I am grateful to You for the good times I enjoyed with them. However, it is not wise for me to dwell on the past and to keep looking back. My eternal Lord and Savior, help me realize and appreciate anew each day that my future is in Your hands.

Lord, You know all things and You know how much I need new friends. Help me see that in order to gain a friend I must be a friend. Help me be considerate of others. Assist me so I might respect the rights and the opinions of others. Keep me from being overly critical of others, while at the same time do not permit me to think too highly of myself. Help me love my neighbor as I love myself.

I am asking for Your help because I realize I am not a spiritual island, and I need others to help me live for Jesus. I need real Christian friends who will build me up in my trust in You. I need brothers and sisters in the faith with whom I can serve You with gladness.

At the same time, I give myself to You, Jesus, with the prayer that You will use me to build up others in their faith and life in You. In Your saving name I pray. Amen.

I Worry

O Lord, I am worried.
    I am worried about ________________________ .
    I am worried about so many things.
    I admit I have not always put my trust in You.
    I recognize such worry is not consistent with my faith
       in You.
My Father, forgive me for Jesus' sake. Amen.

    (Now look at Matthew 6:25-33. See what God has done for all His creatures. Note also what He would have us do, especially in verse 33. Then turn to 1 Peter 5:7 and act on it.)

Contemplating Suicide*

Holy God, life can be so hard in this world of sin.
    I have failed so often that evrything seems futile.
    There are so many things to do and so little time.

Even though I try hard, I never get finished.
I have so many questions for which I never get
  answers.
I have so many nagging problems for which I never
  find solutions.
O God, I am so confused.
I am so frustrated with life.
I am so inept at living.
I am such a failure.
I look around and see so many people who seem happy.
I see so many people who appear to be well-adjusted,
  while at the same time I am so unhappy and so out
  of place.
And then, my Lord, I wonder:
Why am I here?
What use am I?
What good am I?
Why am I alive?
Why, Lord? Why?
Omniscient God, You know I have wondered whether I
  should continue living.
Since I am such a good-for-nothing, why should I take up
  space in Your world? You know I have been tempted to
  speed up the schedule of my life. I have thought about
  ending it all. In the past You have provided a way out. O
  Lord, help me see the way out now.
But You are also all-compassionate.
Please accept me, Jesus, and please forgive me.
Please accept me, Jesus, and change my image of myself.
Please accept me, Jesus, and give me the confidence to rely
  on You as my only hope and my only salvation.
Please accept me, Jesus, and deliver me from the evil one.
O Jesus, help me, for I know I cannot make it on my own.
  Amen.

---

* Suggested by a resident assistant who worked with such a student.

The Future

When I look at the universe, the work of Your hands, my
    almighty Creator, I wonder:
    Who am I?
    Why do You care for me?
    What shall I do?
    What should be my goal in life?
    What will I be?
Yet, even as I wonder, I am aware that:
    You made all things and they reflect Your glory.
    You made all things for the benefit of the creatures You
        originally made in Your own image.
    You, in the beginning, regarded what You had created
        as good, very good.
    You made so many things, and yet You keep track of
        everything You have made.
    You still care for the lilies of the field, the birds of the
        air, and the hairs on my head.
    You are a majestic God and a loving Father at the same
        time.
Since You care for such seemingly insignificant things as
lilies, birds, hairs, I know You care for me. You demonstrated Your care in Jesus. And so it is in Him that I
commit myself to You. I trust You, my Father and my
God. My future is in Your hands. Turn my faith to the
future and give me a lively hope. In Jesus, my Life and
my Hope, I pray. Amen.

A General Prayer

Most kind and very gracious Father, thank You
    for being my Father,
    for adopting me into Your family,

for sending Your Son to save me,
for pouring out Your Spirit on me, and
for giving me life everlasting.

However, as You know, I have
many fears and worries,
many doubts and questions.

Some of the questions I have are:
What will happen to me when my "carefree" college
days are over?
Will I be able to find a job?
Where will I live?
With whom will I live?
Whom do You have in mind for me to marry?

I also hold many things dear. I have good friends I will
miss.
I have hopes and dreams.
I have plans and desires.
I have aspirations.

But I want to know what You have in mind for me.
O Lord, please show me the way.
Please lead me in the way You would have me go.
Please guide me to do Your will.
Please help me do all I can to make Your kingdom come.

I ask You to give me
the wisdom to see Your hand at work in my life,
the patience to wait for You,
the strength to do what You set before me,
the courage to dare what is impossible with people but
not with You,
the love to care for the unloved,
the words to speak in behalf of those who cannot speak
for themselves,

and the boldness, even in the face of indifference and
    opposition,
    to trust and obey You.
All such I would do to Your glory in Jesus' wonderful name.
    Amen.

Newly Confirmed

God of grace, I am so grateful to You for sending Your
Spirit into my heart so that I too can confess Jesus as my
Lord. It is great to belong to You and to carry the family
name of Christian. With my new brothers and sisters I am
enjoying the full forgiveness, the enduring peace, and the
real joy of living in and for Jesus. It is wonderful to walk by
faith.

Now, Father of mercy, give me the wisdom to continue
in Jesus' Word so that I will continue to be Jesus' disciple.
Bless the tie that binds me to the family of believers. With
Your Word of truth, my Father, keep me free to serve You all
my days in Jesus' name. It is in His wonderful name that I
address You. Amen.

Non-Christian Parents

Dear everlasting Father, I am so happy that you have
adopted me into Your forever family. You did so purely out
of fatherly divine goodness and mercy. By Your Spirit
alone I know Your mercy in the person of Jesus Christ. I am
happy in Jesus.

But, my Lord, my happiness is not complete. I love my
mom and dad, but I am very concerned about them. As You

are aware, they do not realize that they need Your mercy. As a result they have not accepted the full and free forgiveness You have offered them in Your eternal Son, Jesus. I am unhappy that they have not been born again. Please send Your Spirit to my mom and dad. By the Law convict them of their sins. Then, by the Gospel, convert them to Your grace.

I offer myself to You, eternal Father, as one who would witness to my earthly parents. Grant that my witness be done with love and respect. Help me honor my father and my mother as I bring them the Good News. I want them to be with us in heaven. I have learned it is Your will that none be lost and all people come to the knowledge of their salvation in Christ Jesus. As a result of such knowledge, I am certain You want my earthly mother and father to be saved also. O Lord, send Your light and salvation to my parents. Father, hear me.
Spirit, help me.
Jesus, intercede for me. Amen.

For Non-Christians

Thank You very much, my Father, for giving eternal life to me in the person of Jesus Christ. I praise You for the undeserved favor You have poured out on me in Jesus. With Him, You have given meaning to my life. I now wish to serve You forever.

As I serve You, dear Savior, I see so many people who are living only for themselves. They live only for themselves because they do not know You. They do not know about Your love, Your forgiveness, and Your peace. I am concerned about these people. I recognize that Your Spirit has put this concern in my heart.

Now by the same Spirit, dear Jesus, move me to do

things and to speak words to these people so they will see there is more to life than meets the eye. Use me, dear Father, to show my unbelieving friends they need Your forgiveness and that they can have it in Jesus.

> "Lord, lay some soul upon my heart
> And love that soul through me;
> And may I gladly do my part
> To lead that soul to Thee!"

In Jesus' saving name I pray. Amen.

For the Holy Spirit

Spirit of the Lord, rest on me as You rested on Jesus.
> Fill me with Yourself.
> Fill me up to overflowing with love for Jesus.
> Make me a winsome witness of Your grace and peace.

Spirit of the living God, fall on me with Your wisdom and power. Grant that I may delight in the fear of the Lord.

Spirit of Truth, counsel me not only to be wise unto my salvation in Jesus, but also prudent in the use of all the gifts You have given me.

Spirit of the Father and of the Son, deepen my dedication to Jesus and give me boldness and perseverance in His service. Amen.

Helping Others

Lord of hosts, You have been my Helper.
> You have helped me with my greatest problem.
> You have taken away my sin.
> You have relieved me of my guilt.
> You have taken away the punishment I deserve
> > because of my sin and my guilt.

You have given me the gift of eternal life.
All this You have done for me in Jesus Christ.
What greater Helper could I have?
Lord of my life, so rule in my heart and in my life
    that I will willingly and cheerfully help
        those whom I meet today.
Overcome my reluctance to become involved
    with those who are in need.
Overrule the fear I have of helping others,
    especially those in trouble.
Use me, Lord, to love others in thought, word, and deed as
    You have loved me.
Send Your Spirit so that I can give myself
    to Jesus and His service., Amen.

Love

Lord of life and God of love, You have taught me in Your Word that love is the fulfillment of Your holy Law. I have learned that You want me to love You and serve You with all I am and have. You also want me to love my neighbor the way I love myself.

My Lord and my God, this is hard to do. It is very difficult for me to love the way You want me to love. I realize I never, even at my best moments, seem to measure up to Your expectations. My Father, I am sorry I have disappointed You so often. Please forgive me. I truly want to obey and please You.

It is great to know that Jesus, Your perfect Son, fulfilled Your Law given in the Ten Commandments to the letter. He did so for me. He did so because He loves me. This is amazing, since I do not always love myself. Fill me, my

Father, with the Spirit of Jesus, so I will be able to love others as Jesus has loved me.

Your love, my Jesus, is perfect. It is unselfish. By it You demonstrated You were not afraid to get involved with people who really needed Your love. You got so involved that You were hurt, and yet You did not hold back. You gave Your all.

Jesus, Lover of my soul, let me love others. Help me really share the burdens, the hurts, and the troubles of others. Let me not only rejoice with those who rejoice but cry with those who cry. Guide me by Your Spirit to open myself to others and to offer myself in loving service to them without fear of being used. Lead me to serve others as freely and as sincerely as You have served me. In Your name of wondrous love, my Jesus, I pray. Amen.

Guidance While Dating

Father, how am I supposed to know when "the right one" comes along? Will You please tell me how I will know him/her? When I go out on a date I wonder if this is the one You have in mind for me to marry. However, sooner or later I have been disappointed. Have my standards been too high? Are they higher than Your requirements? Do I have too high an opinion of myself? I wonder if by saving myself for "the right one" it might mean I will be left over for no one.

Perhaps I have been looking at others too critically. Guide me, Father, to look more critically at myself. Help me to develop attitudes and skills that will be respected by others. Help me make myself attractive both on the inside and on the outside. Teach me to manage my time and my finances carefully. Assist me to be more considerate of others so I will be a good team member in my future marriage. Prepare me so I might prepare myself to be a good and faithful husband/wife. Fill my mind with good thoughts.

Then, my Father, bring into my life the person You have in mind to be my husband/wife. Join us together in holy matrimony and keep us together until one of us dies. Until I find that person, keep me from being impatient. Grant me patience in Jesus. Amen.

Before a Date

Great and gracious God, I appreciate the opportunities I have to speak to You about matters of concern to me.

Tonight I am going out on a date with ________________ . He/she is a nice person. He/she is a Christian. I am looking forward to having a good time with him/her. Guide us during the time You give us together to be Your faithful children. Bless us so we may be a blessing to each other. Help us to express our regard for each other with respect. Make us wise enough so we will not do anything about which we will later be ashamed. May the time we spend with each other draw us closer together.

Please guard us with Your angels both as we go and as we return. It is in Jesus, our Brother, that I pray. Amen.

For Sexual Purity

Lord Jesus, I am so tempted to sin sexually. Others do not understand when I try to obey Your commandment: "Do not commit adultery."

Lord Jesus, be my Forgiveness when I sin, my Strength when I am tempted, and my Guide when I am at a loss as to what I should think and do. Teach me to use both the shield of faith for protection and the sword of the spirit for attacking the forces of evil that say sex outside of marriage is okay.

Heavenly Bridegroom, fill my mind with the realization that my sexual nature is noble and for noble use. Fill me with your Spirit of truth so that I will not abuse the gift of sex. Help me keep myself pure so that I will be able to give myself as a holy bride/groom to the one You have in mind for me to marry.

Oh my Savior, the sexual pressures of the day are so great; I need Your help. I approach You with boldness for help in this time of need. Jesus, please hear me and help me. Amen.

Looking Forward
to Marriage

Father, You know how much I am looking forward to entering marriage with Your blessing. Bless _______________ and me as we prepare for married life. Help us understand each other better each day. Let our love and our commitment to each other grow. Increase our thoughtfullness and consideration for each other. Build our respect for each other, Lord; make us the best of friends even before we marry.

Jesus, increase our faith so that as we draw closer to You we will draw closer to each other. Then, when we are no longer two but one, give us joy as joint heirs of the grace of eternal life which is ours in You. Teach us true love by guiding us to submit ourselves to each other out of reverence for You.

We pray even as we would live in Your name, O Jesus. Amen.

Student Leader's Prayer

Jesus, my Leader and my Lord.

Thank You for the opportunity to serve You and others in the position of leadership to which I have been elected. I am overwhelmed by the vote of confidence others have given me. I know I cannot make it on my own: I need Your support, Your encouragement, Your counsel, and Your guidance.

Help me, Lord, so that I may view my election as an opportunity to serve You and enrich the lives of others. Do not let me force my will on others. Give me and those I lead a spirit of cooperation and mutual respect. Help us trust and love one another.

When there are differences of opinion among us, show us how to disagree without being disagreeable. Counsel us so that we may resolve our differences in such a way that we may do something rather than nothing. Grant, my Lord, that what we do will please You and help those whom we serve. When my co-workers and I encounter disappointments, teach us to rely even more on You than we have in the past. Help us view problems and even failures as new opportunities to serve.

As long as I hold this leadership position, give me the counsel of Your Spirit of truth. Never let me compromise Your truth. Deliver me from all temptations to abuse the power I have been given as a leader.

Jesus, heavenly Leader, lead Thou on. Amen.

Student Athlete's Prayer

Lord Creator, accept my praise for the strength and the coordination You have given me. Because of this strength and coordination I am able to compete in intercollegiate athletics. As Your child by faith in Christ Jesus, I always want to be your man/woman even on the field of competition.

At the start of this competition I commit myself to You. Please take care of me and those against whom I compete. Give me the concentration I need to block out all distractions so I will perform to the best of my ability. Make it possible for me to use all my mental and physical energies in such a way that I will perform as well as I am able.

When I have given my all, give me a sense of satisfaction about what I have done. If I succeed, keep me humble enough not to give the glory to myself but to You alone. If I lose, help me learn from the loss and continue to do the best I can.

I trust in Jesus, whom I know as the One who has gone before me into Your presence, Father. He has prepared the way for me. In Him I am confident that I can stand before You and receive from You a victory prize that will never fade away. Amen.

So Busy

Dearest Lord Jesus, forgive me for being so busy these days that I have not stopped to thank and praise You. I am sorry I have been taking You and what You have done for me for granted. Forgive me for putting You in the backseat instead of the driver's seat of my life.

I'll admit I enjoy school. I enjoy being busy. I thrive on activity, and I am happiest when I have plenty to do. But I am sorry I have gotten so wrapped up in what I am doing that I have forgotten You.

I ask You to forgive me.
Create in me a clean heart . . .
     and put a new and right spirit within me.
Cast me not away from Your presence.
     and take not Your Holy Spirit from me.
Restore to me the joy of Your salvation.
(Psalm 51:10-12)

Please, Lord, give me opportunities in the future to put You first in my life. Give me another chance to show how grateful I am to You. Lord Jesus, I live and I pray in You alone. Amen.

When I Make Music

Creative Father, thank You very much for the musical talent You have given me. Music is an important part of me, Lord, and there is nothing I enjoy more than praising You through its beautiful sounds.

Beautiful Savior, I want to praise You with the talent I have. I want to share Your love through my music. Use what I offer to build others up in their trust in You.

Wise Counselor, make me intelligent in the use of my talent. Guide me in such a way that I will never seek my own glory when I make music. Keep me from merely performing.

My God, always give me a song to sing and music to play for You.

Let me forever sing a new song to You, O Lord.

Make my life a song of praise, Hallelujah, in Jesus. Amen.

Working While at College

God the Father almighty, maker of heaven and earth as well as all things visible and invisible, I believe and confess that You are not retired but are still working. You are upholding all things by Your Word of power. You have done and continue to do marvelous works.

As a child whom You have adopted by grace in Christ Jesus, I am grateful to You for giving me many opportunities to use my interests and my talents. At this time I am particularly grateful to You for permitting me to work while I am attending school. I thank and praise You for helping me find a job by which I can support myself while I am a student.

My dear Father, never let me take my job for granted. Never let me take for granted any of the daily bread You give me. Bless me so I may be a blessing to those I work for and with. As You do, grant that I may develop into a responsible, productive, and respected citizen of this community. In addition, grant that I may not grow tired of serving others, and that I may serve You and those You love as faithfully as You have served me in Your beloved Son.

In Jesus, in whom I trust as my Savior and my Lord, I praise You and seek Your blessing. Amen.

Peace

God of justice and love, I praise You for the reconciliation You have effected between Yourself and all of us who were Your enemies. You accomplished that reconciliation through the blood of Jesus Christ. He is my Peace.

Lord of hosts, You want peace on earth, but there are wars and rumors of wars. We do not have peace on earth because nations, like individuals, are sinful and selfish. We humans are guilty of inhumanity to man. Father, forgive us and heal us.

Comfort all the victims of war. Punish all who do evil (Romans 13:4). Guide us always to seek peace and pursue it. Cause all wars to cease, and let justice reign on earth. Move us to love our enemies and to do good to those who hate us. Conquer all Your enemies with Your love in Jesus, the Prince of Peace. I pray in His name. Amen.

Thanks

Amen. Thank You, Lord.

Thanks, for the amazing, exciting, and wonderful world You have given to me.

Thanks for the blessings, both great and small, which You pour down on me every day.

Thanks for the joys and the sorrows, the laughter and the tears.

Thanks for making me the unique individual I am.

You knew me from the moment of my conception.

You counted my members even before my parents knew I existed.

Thanks for giving me life.

And *eternal* thanks for remaking me by Your grace through Baptism. Thank You, Lord. Amen.

Thanks for Gifts
Taken for Granted

My Creator and my God, as I lie here now I am thinking about all the wonderful things You have given me. Most of the time I take those gifts for granted.

O Lord, You have blessed me beyond many of my contemporaries. You have blessed me with the ability to see, hear, taste, smell, and touch. I am able to talk to You and others. I am in great health. My brothers and sisters love me, and my parents are tops. I even have friends who would die for me. I have been permitted to go to college, and I am now looking forward to graduating. I have never gone hungry, and I have always had a roof over my head and clothes on my back. I have enjoyed many pleasures in this life. But, best of all, You have given Your very best, Your only Son to be my Savior. In Him I am enjoying the abundant life, and will do so forevermore.

So often I have taken these gifts for granted and have forgotten to thank You, the Giver, for them. Forgive me, O Lord, for Jesus' sake.

Give me the wise counsel of Your Spirit so that in the future I will be more appreciative, and help me find a way to share my blessings with the less fortunate.

May the words of my mouth and the meditation of my heart be acceptable to You, my Jesus. Amen.

Thanks for a Place to Live

Dear Father, our eternal Shelter. I thank You for:
     this dormitory/apartment,
     the roof that keeps out the heat of summer
     and the cold of winter,
     the temperature controls that give me comfort
     even when it's uncomfortable outside,
     the blessing of hot and cold running water,
     the comfort of my bed, desk, chairs,
     and dresser.
Forgive me for:
     Lack of appreciation of the many comforts
       that are provided,
     abusing this living space,
     ignoring the actions of those who vandalize
       this building.
     Protect each of us who live here from dangers by fire, storm, and other disasters.
     I ask this as Your child by faith in Jesus Christ. Amen.

Thanks for Spiritual Armor

Lord of hosts, the commander-in-chief of the angel armies, I hail You for the evidences of Your might, Your mercy, and Your wisdom which I have seen.

I thank and praise You for the armor and the weapons You have issued to me so that I am able to stand against rather than fall to the devil. Thanks for giving me:
the shield of faith,
the sword of the Spirit, which is the Word of God,

the holy Christian church, the communion of saints,
loving parents and siblings,
faithful pastors and teachers,
pious and faithful rulers,
good Christian literature and music,
as well as Gospel radio and television programs.

I recognize with gratitude that such equipment is not only provided for my protection but also for my nurture in the faith.

Jesus, into Your hands I commend my spirit. Amen.

Pressures to Conform

Jesus, You know how it feels to live in this world. It is not easy for me to follow You while I am living with so many people who only live for themselves. The pressures to conform are so great; it would be so easy to give in. Jesus, at times I am so weak. I get so confused about what is right and wrong, about what is moral and immoral, and about what is pleasing and displeasing to You.

I must also admit, to my sorrow, that I have not always been strong in You, Lord. I have given in to temptations in my thoughts, in my words, and in my actions. I have not always been a good witness for You. I have not always produced the fruits of faith which will move others to glorify our Father in heaven. For such conformity to the world I am truly sorry. I sincerely ask You to forgive me. I also ask You to fill me with Your strong Spirit so that I may change my sinful thoughts, words, and actions.

Please transform me by renewing my mind and renovating my actions. Since it is Your will that I live in this world and serve You where You have sent me, I am bold enough to ask You to equip me with Your Spirit and Your Word. Let me demonstrate in my words and actions the victory You have given me. Let me show others how great it is to be more than a conqueror through You who love me. Let me always say and show the truth of my praise: "Thanks be to God, who gives us the victory through our Lord Jesus Christ." Amen.

For Revival of Faith

Jesus, my heart is not lifted up. I am not experiencing the joy of my salvation which You promised. O Lord, tell me what is wrong.

I recall with fondness the days when You lifted me up to heights of spiritual joy. I know there were times when I rejoiced in You with my whole heart and with all that was within me. I remember the times when I was really excited to live every new day for Jesus.

What has happened to me, Lord?

Why do I feel so spiritually weak?

What is wrong with me?

Ah, I think I know. Your Spirit is at work in me convicting me of my sin. I admit I have not continued in You, Lord Jesus. My faith has become weak because I have not fed it with the good spiritual food You provide in Your Word. I am ashamed to admit that it has been a long time since I have accepted Your invitation to dine at Your table.

Jesus, my Good Shepherd, lead me again to the green pastures of Your Word. Feed me so I may grow stronger. Bless me from Your Word so I will know the truth and be free. I pray that You renew me and revive my faith. Jesus, hear me. Amen.

About a New Roommate

Father, Son, and Holy Spirit, Hallelujah!

I come to You, Lord, because I am concerned about who will be my roommate. I am worried about what kind of person he/she might be. Forgive me, Lord, for the judgments (prejudices) I have formed in my mind about my roommate before I even met him/her. Forgive me also for not talking to You about this sooner.

Grant me Your vision of the future. Give me confidence in the realization that my time is in Your good hands. Help me look forward to the good times I will have with my roommate. Make me wise enough to see any troubles and difficulties as opportunities for us to share Your forgiving and edifying love with each other.

Make me a good roommate. Give me the mind of Christ so I can show my roommate respect and consideration. Make me dependable, responsible, and helpful.

If my new roommate is not a Christian, send the Holy Spirit to me so I can bear witness to Your saving grace with sincerity, joy, and gentleness in Jesus. Amen.

In Sickness

My heavenly Physician, I've been sitting here wondering if You know how rotten I feel. I have been sick for so long. I am sure that I look at least as bad as I feel. I certainly do not want anybody to see me this way.

Lord, forgive me for my puny faith.

I commit myself to You.

I believe in You.

I depend on You.

I need You every hour.
Oh, how I need You!
Have mercy on me, Jesus, and heal me. Amen.

Another Prayer in Sickness

O Jesus, the Great Physician, I am *so* sick, and I am sick and tired of being sick. I come to You because I know You can heal me. I come to You because I remember that You have invited all who are weak and heavy laden to come to You. The Gospels report that You laid Your hands on many people and healed them of various diseases. As I come to You I am confident that, if it is Your will for me, You can make me well again.

My Lord and Savior, I have been sick for so long that things have really piled up on me. I have so much home-work to do, and so much to catch up on, but I don't feel like studying. O Jesus, help me and heal me so I do not get any further behind.

I submit myself and my needs to You, O Lord. I am confident You hear me and that You will do what is best for me. Please help me and heal me in Your own way and in Your own time. In all circumstances in life, teach me to seek first Your kingdom and Your righteousness. I am certain that You will give me all the things I need. Let Your will be done in my life.

Hear me, O God, as I depend on You and pray to You in Jesus' name. Amen.

For a Sick Student

Lord, I worship You as my eternal Father. You are the Savior of my soul and the Lord of my life. With all who trust in Jesus, I love and honor You.

Please hear my prayers in behalf of _______________
_______________ . He/She is very sick. Please heal him/her.
Don't let him/her get any worse. He/She hasn't been able to
go to class for a week. _______________ is falling
behind in his/her school work, and the end of the semester
is not too far off. Lord, Great Physician, You know all these
things. I want You to know that I am concerned about
him/her. I add my prayers for healing to his/hers. I do so
without demanding anything of You. I am only submitting
my requests to You. I am beseeching You to help
_______________ according to Your good pleasure.

I am praying with full confidence that You will hear me
in Jesus' name. Amen.

On the Death of a Friend

Hey, God, what about the death of _______________ ?
My friend was only ____ years old. He/She was too young to
die. He/She was the same age as I am! Why did You let this
happen? Why? Why now? Why, Lord, why?

I'm sorry, Lord. I know I should not question You and
what You do or permit. Forgive me for thinking that things
must be as I think. Forgive me for only thinking of myself
and my own feelings.

I know _______________ was ready to meet You. I
praise You for bringing my friend to the saving knowledge
of Your Son, Jesus. I also thank You for the good things
he/she did for me and others while he/she served You here
below.

I intercede with You in behalf of _______________'s
parents, loved ones, and friends. Comfort them and support
them during these sad days. Let them remember how
_______________ trusted in Jesus and lived by faith

in Him. Permit us all to remember him/her as a sincere follower of Jesus.

Make me aware, by this experience with death, of the brevity of life here on earth. Teach me to watch and pray and to be a faithful steward of all the days You give me. In the end, grant that I may die Your people's death and live and reign with You forevermore.

I commit myself in this prayer to Jesus, who conquered sin and death for me and who is the Lord of my life. Amen.

Help with a Special Project

O Lord, I recognize and praise You as my exciting, wonder-filled, thoughtful, and caring God. I am so pleased that I can look to You and come to You with all my concerns.

Right now I am very concerned about doing a good job on this special project. Bless my efforts. Give me the creativity to design the project in such a way that it will reflect both the unity and the diversity which are characteristics of both You and Your creation. Enable me to execute skillfully the design I devise, so that what I produce will be beautiful, as You are beautiful. Give me the persistence to complete it and get it in on time.

When this special project is finished, remind me to give You the glory, O God, in Jesus' name. Amen.

At an Academic Crossroad

Here I am again, Lord. Please hear me and help me as You did before. I am standing at another academic crossroad. You know how frustrated I feel when I do not know which way to go. There are so many majors available, and there are so many courses from which to choose. I am not certain what I should do. I am afraid the choice I might make will take me down the wrong road. I am afraid of going off in the wrong direction. I am worried about getting stuck with courses I won't like, as well as course work that will bore me.

O my Father, even in academic life I want to be Your faithful son/daughter. I want to please You. I want You to be proud of me and my accomplishments. But I am not always certain what You want me to do.

Please do not think I am ungrateful. I do recognize that You have blessed me while I have been a student. More than that, You have blessed me with Your eternal love, full forgiveness, and enduring peace in Jesus. Remind me often of what You have done, are doing, and will do for me. Give me courage to face the future. Renew in me the confidence that nothing will ever separate me from Your love.

Now give me the courage and the confidence to choose one of the roads. Jesus, lead Thou on. Amen.

Preparing to Study Abroad

My Father in heaven, I thank and praise You for giving me the opportunity to study abroad next semester. I am so grateful to You because I know many people do not even have the opportunity to go to college much less to go to school in a foreign country. I am so excited! Help me, Lord, to show my excitement in such a way that my friends will not think I am bragging about myself. Help me always to give glory to You alone.

Even though I am so thankful and so excited, I must admit I have some mixed emotions. I am a bit afraid. It will be hard to leave my good friends here on campus. I am so comfortable and secure here. I know I will not be as comfortable or as secure in a new and strange country. Assure me now and reassure me later that though people, places, and things change, You do not change. Remind me always of the truth that You will be my ever-present Help in every trouble, in every place, and at every time.

All-knowing Father, make me wise enough to use the new experiences which are ahead of me so that I will mature in mind and spirit. While I am away from home, make me friendly so I might make new friends. Let my investment in this study abroad show dividends in my life.

O Father, I am really looking forward to the good things You have in store for me in the months ahead. I commit myself to You in Jesus' redeeming name. Amen.

Before Serving an Internship

I am so grateful to You, Lord my God, for providing me with the internship I am about to start. Oh, I know it was arranged through the college and through the company for which I will work, but I am confident You guided the process all along the way. I know You are the One from whom all my blessings flow.

Bless me in the work I will do so that I will be a blessing to those with whom and for whom I work. Make me a faithful worker. Give me wisdom when I am in doubt. Give me perseverance when I am hard-pressed. Support me with Your love when I try to do what is right and what is pleasing to You.

As I serve this internship, I wish to be a good representative of my college. I would also like to serve well so others might see that one who is dedicated to Jesus can be an intelligent and productive member of society.

My Lord, I want to be Your faithful ambassador. Help me in Jesus' name. Amen.

A Student Teacher Prays

Dear heavenly Father, I am sorry, for I have gone through another day of student teaching without thinking very much about You. I have depended only on myself. I have enjoyed some success, but I have also suffered failures. When I have succeeded, I have taken credit for what I did. When I have failed, I have blamed others. Forgive me, Lord. Forgive me for thinking only about myself. Forgive me for forgetting about You and what You want me to do.

Tonight I ask You to bless my study and preparation for tomorrow's classes and then give me a good night's sleep. If it is Your will, give me another day. Give me new opportunities to serve You and my students. Permit me to witness, in word and deed, to how wonderful it is to be Your child.

Hear me, Father, for I pray in my Brother Jesus' name. Amen.

Before a Job Interview

God the Father Almighty, I recognize and praise You for the wonderful job You did in designing and constructing the vast universe in which we live, and especially the beautiful blue marble on which we live. You do beautiful work.

Now, my Father, I am looking forward to the opportunities I will have when I enter the working world. I am anxious to do something with my education. It seems I have always been studying and preparing. I know I have been working toward a day like this since I began school, but now I am frightened. I am afraid I will not do well during the job interview.

O God, my Refuge, be my Strength and my Help, so I might make a correct impression and give a good accounting of what I have learned to the _________________________ Company's personnel officer. Help me to relax and be myself. If it is Your will, give the interviewer the insight and the foresight to see me as an employee who will be a hard worker and one who will make significant contributions to the company's future. Above all, grant me an effective and winsome testimony that in all I do I serve You and want to serve others in Jesus' name.

Father, for this job interview and for my whole life, I commend myself to You in Jesus' name. Amen.

After a Job Interview

Dear Father in heaven, I recognize that You provide Your children with many and varied gifts. Please make me a faithful steward of those gifts You have entrusted to me.

I give thanks to You for the opportunity I was given to demonstrate my talents to the personnel people from the _________________________ Company. I pray that they were able to see I could be an asset to their organization.

If it is Your will, please guide the company to offer me a position. If I receive such an offer give me the wisdom to know whether or not I should accept it. Should the company decide not to offer me a job, help me learn from the interview process.

I ask You to hear me, Father, as I pray in Jesus' name. Amen.

On Receiving Job Offers

God the Father, Source of all knowledge and wisdom, accept the praise I offer You for the truths You have made known to us through Your holy Word. You were the One who made Solomon such a wise man. It was to Your glory that he used his knowledge and wisdom. When I think of wise men I cannot help but remember the difficult issues people like Solomon were able to resolve with Your help.

I, Your child by faith in Christ Jesus, am now facing some difficult questions. I have been offered positions with the _________________________ Company, with the _________ ______________ Company, and with the _______________________ Company. Lord, what do You want me to do? I must make a choice soon.

My Lord, give me the wisdom to ask questions that will help me arrive at a decision pleasing to You. Guide those questions to the right people. Give me the wisdom to listen carefully to the answers given. Please help me choose the job in which I can use the talents You have given me to Your glory.

I speak to You, my Father, in the name of the One who always pleased You and who now occupies the position at Your right hand, Jesus Christ. Amen.

When
Christians
Pray Together

Praise the Lord!
Praise God in His sanctuary;
    praise Him in His mighty firmament! . . .
Let everything that breathes praise the Lord!
Praise the Lord!

Psalm 150:1, 6

At the Beginning of a Meeting

We address You, our God, who preside over all that You have created, with confidence that You are present with us when we call on You. Bless us at this meeting of ______________ ____________ (name of group). Give us Your wisdom so we will all think, say, and do only those things which are pleasing to You. Guide all who are present to ask appropriate questions, to listen with open minds, to draw conclusions based on fact, and to lay plans that will be useful to all affected by the actions of this group. Grant us Your Spirit of truth and holiness, our Father, so we might deliberate and even disagree in love without becoming disagreeable.

O Lord, our Lord, deliver us from the evil one. Do not let the author of all confusion and the father of lies lurk among us. We pray, even as we begin this meeting, in Jesus' name. Amen.

At the Close of a Meeting

Lord God, Creator and Sustainer of all good things, we thank You for the productive meeting we have just concluded. We appreciate very much that You have given us so many talented people to serve ______________________ (name of group). Thanks for giving us this opportunity to serve You and to serve others in Jesus' name.

We praise You for guiding us as we worked through the agenda. We glorify You for enabling us to devise a common plan of action without having been disagreeable.

We now ask, if it is Your will, that our plan of action succeed and that we may all support the decisions we have made with both our words and our deeds. Thereby deepen our commitment to each other. Help us fulfill our responsibilities.

Should our decisions and plans prove unpopular to those we wish to serve, do not let us become defensive. Keep us mindful that, as fallible human beings, we are not above criticism. Help us accept criticism with grace. Keep us humble, Lord.

Should our decisions and plans be misunderstood, guide us to explain how we reached the decisions and devised the plans we did, based on the facts available to us. Help us articulate with care and consideration how we drew our conclusions and laid our plans with everyone's best interests in mind.

We address You in prayer, Lord God, because we know and confess that Jesus Christ lives to make intercession for us. Amen.

At the Beginning
of Bible Study

Dear Father, You are the Source of all truth and the Giver of all wisdom. As we worship You, we ask You to be present with us as we study together the words You have had written in the Bible for our learning.

Bless our leader so that he/she will help us see the wonderful things You have stored for us in the section of the Bible we are about to study. Guide each of us, Spirit of truth, so that we may see how the passages fit together and how they edify us in a way no human wisdom can. Enable us to share our various experiences and insights so our oneness in Jesus will not be broken down but built up.

As we open Your book, open our hearts and minds so we might enjoy our Bible study. Renew in us the joy of our salvation so that we will build each other up in our trust in You, our commitment to Jesus, and our willingness to follow the guidance of Your Spirit.

We thank You, Lord, for this opportunity to study together, and we thank You for all our friends here today. We do so in the name of the One who has made us brothers and sisters, Jesus the Christ. Amen.

At the Close of Bible Study

Father of mercy and God of grace, by means of Your holy Word You have again revived our faith. You keep Your Word; You are a faithful God.

As we have opened our hearts and our minds to Your truth and grace, we now ask You to guide us to open our lives, our hands, and our mouths so we will be effective witnesses for Jesus in this world. Help us share what we have learned with those around us, especially those who do not know what a merciful and faithful God You are.

Be with us as we leave this special group of people. Watch between us as we go our separate ways. If it is Your pleasure, bring us back together again. By Your grace alone we are together in Jesus. Amen.

Before Meals

Our Father who art in heaven, we hallow Your name, because You have again fulfilled Your promise to give us our daily bread. Before we eat the food before us:

We thank You for the farmers who worked the soil, planted the seeds, and harvested the crops.

We thank You for those who transported the crops from the fields to the processors and from the processors to our stores.

We thank You for all the cooks, servers, and organizers of this meal.

We now ask that this food will be a blessing to us and that through our use of it we will be a blessing to others. Help us also to remember those who are not so fortunate as we and who suffer hunger.

Bless our fellowship, Father, as we break this bread together.

We address You in the name of Jesus. He is the Bread of Life. He feeds our souls that we hunger no more. Amen.

After Meals

Dear God and Father, we thank and praise You for the meal we have just enjoyed together. Bless now the use to which we put what we have eaten. Bless also that which has been left over, so nothing of Your good gifts may be wasted.

Thanks also for the friends both old and new with whom we have dined. Help our relationship with old friends to deepen and our relationship with new friends to continue to grow.

Bless us now as we return to our rooms and to our studies. Keep us in Your care and equip us both in body and mind to serve You always in Jesus' name. Amen.

Before Participating in a Sporting Event

God, our Father, we are about to compete in a game of _______________________ . We recognize that You are the One who has given us the variety of talents we have as a team. Grant that we will use our abilities in ways which are pleasing to You and pleasing to our brothers and sisters in Christ. Guide the referees to call the game fairly, and give us the spirit of humility to accept their judgments without complaining. Please keep all members of both teams from physical harm. Remind us it is only a game.

As we follow Jesus, the Forerunner of our faith, so we also submit ourselves and our wills to You in His name. Amen.

After a Game by the Winners

Holy Father, we praise You and thank You for the skills and abilities that allowed us to win this game. We are thankful for the opportunity to play, and we ask that You continue to watch over us as we prepare for the next game. Keep our attitude from becoming one of arrogance and pride in our abilities. Continue to send us the Holy Spirit so we may remain on Your team forever. We ask this in the name of Jesus. Amen.

After a Game by the Losers

Holy Father, we praise You and thank You for the opportunity to play this game. We ask that You continue to watch over us as we prepare for the next game. Help us to learn from this loss so we might continue to improve and use our talents to Your glory. Keep our attitude from becoming one of dejection and despondence. Continue to send us the Holy Spirit so we may remain on Your team forever. We ask this in the name of Jesus. Amen.